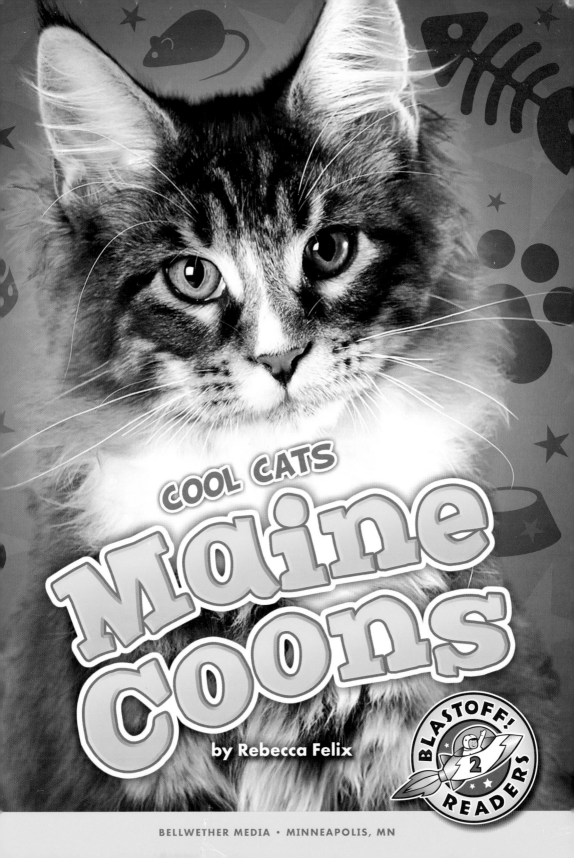

COOL CATS

Maine Coons

by Rebecca Felix

BLASTOFF! READERS 2

BELLWETHER MEDIA • MINNEAPOLIS, MN

Note to Librarians, Teachers, and Parents:

Blastoff! Readers are carefully developed by literacy experts and combine standards-based content with developmentally appropriate text.

Level 1 provides the most support through repetition of high-frequency words, light text, predictable sentence patterns, and strong visual support.

Level 2 offers early readers a bit more challenge through varied simple sentences, increased text load, and less repetition of high-frequency words.

Level 3 advances early-fluent readers toward fluency through increased text and concept load, less reliance on visuals, longer sentences, and more literary language.

Level 4 builds reading stamina by providing more text per page, increased use of punctuation, greater variation in sentence patterns, and increasingly challenging vocabulary.

Level 5 encourages children to move from "learning to read" to "reading to learn" by providing even more text, varied writing styles, and less familiar topics.

Whichever book is right for your reader, Blastoff! Readers are the perfect books to build confidence and encourage a love of reading that will last a lifetime!

This edition first published in 2016 by Bellwether Media, Inc.

No part of this publication may be reproduced in whole or in part without written permission of the publisher. For information regarding permission, write to Bellwether Media, Inc., Attention: Permissions Department, 5357 Penn Avenue South, Minneapolis, MN 55419.

Library of Congress Cataloging-in-Publication Data

Felix, Rebecca, 1984- author.
   Maine Coons / by Rebecca Felix.
      pages cm. – (Blastoff! Readers. Cool Cats)
   Summary: "Relevant images match informative text in this introduction to Maine coon cats. Intended for students in kindergarten through third grade"– Provided by publisher.
   Audience: Ages 5-8
   Audience: K to grade 3
   Includes bibliographical references and index.
   ISBN 978-1-62617-232-6 (hardcover: alk. paper)
   1. Maine coon cat–Juvenile literature. I. Title.
   SF449.M34F45 2016
   636.8'3–dc23

                               2015002471

Printed in the United States of America, North Mankato, MN.

Table of Contents

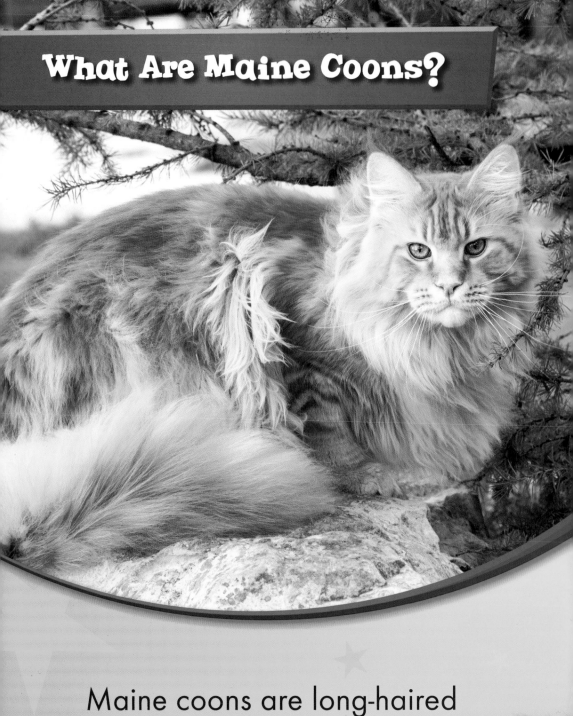

Maine coons are long-haired cats with **bushy** tails.

They are one of the
largest cat **breeds**.

These cats are gentle and loving.

Some **communicate** by making chirping noises.

History of Maine Coons

Maine

N
W · E
S

Maine coons are **native** to the northeastern United States, especially Maine.

There are **legends** about these cats. People once believed they were part raccoon! Many Maine coons have ringed tails.

9

Others say a French queen sent her cats to the United States long ago. They **bred** with native cats to make Maine coons.

Today, these **storied** cats
are popular pets in the
United States.

Maine coons can have more than 75 different **coat** patterns. Many are **solid** or **tabby**.

Maine Coon Coats

solid

tabby

smoke

tortoiseshell

A Maine coon's coat has several lengths. It is longest on the belly.

These cats also have long hair on their large paws. It helps the cats walk on snow.

Long ear hair keeps
their ears warm.

15

Maine coons have the longest whiskers of all cats. Their eyes are usually green, gold, or orange.

Maine Coon Profile

— furry ears

— large body

bushy tail

— furry paws

Weight: 9 to 25 pounds (4 to 11 kilograms)

Life Span: 9 to 15 years

Friendly and At Ease

Maine coons are smart. Many can stand up on their back legs.

However, these cats often act **at ease**. Most usually sit quietly.

Maine coons are friendly to people and animals.

Some like water. They may jump in the shower or play in the kitchen sink!

Glossary

at ease—relaxed, calm, and comfortable

bred—produced offspring

breeds—types of cats

bushy—thick and full

coat—the hair or fur covering an animal

communicate—to make information known

legends—stories from the past that cannot be proven, but that many people believe

native—originally from a specific place

solid—one color

storied—having an interesting history

tabby—a pattern that has stripes, patches, or swirls of colors

To Learn More

AT THE LIBRARY
Fuller, Sandy Ferguson. *My Cat, Coon Cat.*
Yarmouth, Me.: Islandport Press, 2011.

Owen, Ruth. *American Longhairs.* New York, N.Y.:
PowerKids Press, 2014.

White, Nancy. *Maine Coons: Super Big.* New York,
N.Y.: Bearport Pub., 2011.

ON THE WEB
Learning more about
Maine coons is as
easy as 1, 2, 3.

1. Go to www.factsurfer.com.

2. Enter "Maine coons" into the search box.

3. Click the "Surf" button and you will see a
   list of related web sites.

With factsurfer.com, finding more
information is just a click away.

Index

The images in this book are reproduced through the courtesy of: AlexussK, front cover; Mitrofanov Alexander, p. 4; Eric Isselee, pp. 5, 9 (left, right), 13 (top left), 15; Juniors Bildarchiv/ Alamy, p. 6; Linn Currie, p. 7; Gerard Lacz Images/ Superstock, p. 10; gurinaleksandr, p. 11; Mario Kuhnke/ Glow Images, p. 12; Ermolaev Alexander, p. 13 (top right); absolutimages, p. 13 (bottom left); Seregraff, p. 13 (bottom right); DragoNika, p. 14; TalyaPhoto, p. 16; Elena Butinova, p. 17; Adya, p. 18; Christian Htter/ Glow Images, p. 19; Tim Davis/ Corbis, p. 20; eZeePics Studio, p. 21.